Finer Femininity

A Sunshiny Disposition

Spring 2015

Edited and Compiled by

Mrs. Leane G. VanderPutten

DEDICATION

This little periodical is dedicated to all the women in this
world who are devoted to making their families,
their homes, and therefore society,
a beautiful Catholic Masterpiece
in this fallen world.

CONTENTS

ACKNOWLEDGMENTS

Thank you to my husband, Vincent, for being so supportive and encouraging in this endeavor and all through our married life. ☺

1. SPRING HAS SPRUNG!

By Leane VanderPutten

I love this time of the year. The roses will be blossoming out and we are anticipating the blooming of many more flowers as the season progresses!

We haven't always had a yard that looks beautiful. But we have always tried, no matter how hard times were, to eke out a little bit to get some blossoms going. Flowers spread joy and happiness. They are a gift from God and I think they are therapy for the soul.

We lived in a very small, one-bedroom home for ten years. We had seven children in that home. While we lived in this little house, (which many called "the shack") we always had flowers, though not an abundance like we do now. I didn't plant perennials there and I am glad of that so I didn't have to say good-bye to them. We managed somehow to have our little annual flower garden.

I am not known for my green thumb....but I have grown into it. When you invest time and money into something, you learn how to make it work. Flowers mean a lot to us, so my thumb has slowly changed color!!

So...if you can, plant some flowers, nurture them, watch them grow and bloom! It's observing God's handiwork at its finest! Maybe each year you can get a perennial or two so you can enjoy them every growing season and one day have an abundance of easy-to-care-for blossoming smile-makers!

And when the winter months come, get yourself some African Violets or some other plants for the house. They will bring a smile and sunshine to your heart when the wind and snow are mounting outside. :)

This is a picture of our little granddaughter, Sienna, admiring one of our lovely zinnias. Actually, I think she is ready to dismantle it, petal by petal!

I love this quote from My Prayer Book by Father Lasance:

"I have always noticed that wherever you find flowers, no matter whether in a garret or in a palace, it is a pretty sure sign that there is an inner refinement of which the world is not cognizant. I have seen flowers cultivated and cherished by some of the lowest and poorest of people. Where these emblems of purity are found, you may rest assured that they represent a hope, and speak of a goodness of heart not to be found where they are absent."

The earth laughs in flowers.
-Ralph Waldo Emerson

"I'd rather have **ROSES** on my table than **DIAMONDS** on my neck." ~Emma Goldman

"A **MORNING-GLORY** at my window satisfies me more than the **metaphysics of books**." ~Walt Whitman

2. DOES YOUR MARRIAGE NEED WARMING UP?

by Charlotte Siems
www.charlottesiems.com

Marriage is the foundation of the family....more foundational than how you educate your children and where you live. It's the oven that bakes family life. When you're baking a cake, an oven with low or no heat won't create what you want. In the same way, a marriage with low or no priority won't create the home you want.

During the season of life when we had four children under the age of four, it was all too easy to view my husband's needs as just another diaper to change. Those babies grew up and we started the homeschool years while adding another baby to the family every couple of years, so it didn't get any easier to keep our marriage a priority.

We didn't give up. Soon we'll celebrate our 32nd anniversary, and we love each other more than ever.

Wondering how to have a better marriage? Here are some thoughts on keeping your marriage growing during the busy childrearing years:

Cut the excuses for why it's okay to ignore your husband. Yes, I know you're busy and tired and the kids need you.....but you can't put your relationship on a shelf for years and expect it to flourish. When we don't water our tomato plants, they shrivel up and die in the heat, and they sure don't produce any fruit. It's the same with our marriage.

Focus on what is RIGHT for a change. Think about what is good about your marriage, about what your husband is doing well, about the things you excel in as a wife. Don't beat yourself (or your husband) up about what needs to get better. You get more of what you focus on, so focus on the good.

Treat your husband like a man. He's your best friend, but he's not your girlfriend (there's a difference). He's not your servant and he's not incompetent with your kids. He has his way of doing things with them and it is not wrong, it's just different.

Look like a woman. Peek in the mirror. How's the makeup and hair doing? What are you wearing? Of course you'll have your days, but a constant wardrobe of a t-shirt and sweat pants sends a message to yourself and to others.

How we dress does affect us, whether we admit it or not. Men are visual, that's how they were created. Deep down they do care how you look and they're not asking for a size 2 model. When you make an effort to look pretty, it helps them feel loved, believe it or not. All the years I wore a size 22W, my husband thanked me over and over for "fixing up."

Accept your husband for who he is and treat him accordingly. What does this look like? No criticism, no nagging, no disrespect, no "jokes" about his masculinity, no rolling your eyes. Plenty of appreciation, lots of admiration and realizing the truth that there are plenty of women out there who would love to treat him this way.

Step back and evaluate whether some things need to change in your relationship during the busy years of raising children. Change can start with you. Your husband really doesn't even have to know. Nobody likes to be a project. You can change your own attitude and actions, and your tremendous influence as a wife will affect your husband.

See what you can do to turn up the heat in your marriage to create the family life you want!

"*Happily ever after is not a* FAIRY TALE. *It's a* CHOICE."

-*Fawn Weaver*

If your husband no longer opens the car door for you, maybe it's time to make changes. And no, I'm not talking about getting a new husband.

Did you know that "taking a mate for granted" is one of the main reasons there is a 50 percent divorce rate? Don't get caught in that trap.

Step back and make sure you're filling each other's emotional tanks. Appreciation is a choice, so choose to be grateful and express your love. The more you do, the easier it becomes.

-Emilie Barnes,
365 Things Every Woman should Know

3. TEACH YOUR CHILD TO PRAY

How to Raise Good Catholic Children
By Mary Reed Newland

Praying is pretty personal. After all, it's conversation with God, and conversation with someone you love ought to be entirely personal — warm and intimate, full of secrets and praises and declarations of love.

Praying ought to be fun, too, most of the time, because it's our one chance to talk as much as we like and know that we don't bore, that we will be heard, and that everything we say draws us closer to God — which is what He wants and the reason for praying in the first place.

The trouble is that many people think of prayer more as a recitation than as a conversation, and all their lives they speak to God with words that other people have put together for them. They're beautiful words, beautifully put together, and they give great praise.

But it's a big mistake to think that only formal prayers are proper when we speak to the Father who made us, who knows us better than we know ourselves and would like us to come simply, like children, and say what we want to say in our own words.

Once there was a girl who told her confessor, "Father, I try to say the Rosary every night when I'm in bed, but get so involved talking to God that, before I know it, I've fallen asleep. Do you think I'm deliberately allowing myself to be distracted?"

Her confessor laughed. "If you were God," he said, "would you rather have someone talk to you in his own words, or in someone else's? By all means, say your Rosary some other time, but continue your conversations with God, and do stop confusing distraction with mental prayer."

This is the understanding of prayer we can give our children in their earliest years, long before they learn recited prayers, and in this way we give them a pattern of approach to God in prayer that will suit not only their childhood, but all the years of their lives.

Even when they begin to learn formal prayers, in the beginning they have no real understanding of them, and it's a rather bleak start to one's life of prayer to think it must consist of a lot of phrases learned by heart but not understood, which one repeats at certain times because Mother says you must.

The Our Father is the perfect pattern for prayer because when the Apostles asked our Lord how they should pray, He gave this prayer to them.

The Mass contains the same pattern, and both make clear the four aspects of our relation to God: penitent, seeker, beloved, and gratefully blessed.

If our children learn to pray each of these roles, they will have learned the rudiments of all prayer, without which the saints say no progress is possible in the spiritual life.

It would be presumptuous for me to tell someone else how he should pray or what words he should use, because the words one person would choose are rarely the words another would choose, and each person's way is shaped and colored by his tastes, personality, and all the many small differences that make him who he is and not someone else.

Those who have prayer have EVERYTHING, because on that basis God can freely enter their lives and act in them, working the marvels of HIS GRACE.

– Fr. Jacques Philippe

Whatever our **trials and disappointments, harsh situations, failures, and faults,** *prayer makes us rediscover enough strength and hope to take up our lives again with* **TOTAL CONFIDENCE IN THE FUTURE.**

– Fr. Jacques Philippe

4. FIBER, FABRIC & STYLE

By Mary Scheeler

Everything has a name and a place to go. Ladies especially need places to store and catalog any and all items. Photos are sorted by date, canned goods by name and date, files by name or date, etc., everything gets organized into recognizable clusters. Along with these items clothing often falls into a dating system. But instead of keeping them in easily accessible, usable files, clothing through fashion often becomes classified as "dated," "old-fashioned," "a la mode," "chic," "youthful," or "old" among other phrases. In the usage of fashion, this dating system presets the ideals of a current age. It takes all items of clothing from the past to the present and categorizes them by their potential usage to the modern lady.

Clothing is rated by its fiber content, its weave, knit, or lack of one, and its style. Many natural fiber fabrics have given way to the synthetic fabrics. Silk, wool, linen, and cotton are the natural fibers. Then they are woven into recognizable fabrics such as velvets, brocades, suiting, crepe, satin, flannel, fleece, houndstooth, jersey, velour, corduroy, denim, muslin, seersucker, poplin, knits, eyelet, etc. The manufactured fibers are rayon, acetate, nylon, polyester, polyurethane laminate, stretch fibers(lycra), and microfibers(silky peachskin). These fibers can also be translated into the above fabrics. Thus we can have satin made from silk or polyester, suiting made from wool or polyester blends, and knits made again from cotton, silk, or polyester and/or nylon blends. The combinations can be endless especially with advanced technology. The weave can be plain, a twill, denim weave, loosely woven, satin weave, wash and wear, stretch wovens, and the many textures of knits. A lack of weave would refer to leather, suede, skins, or manufactured plastic material. The weights of fabric also come into play depending on the garment being created. There are light weights to heavy weights – the lightweights can be used for summer garments like batistes and heavy weights for winter such as corduroy. Or there are light weight silky satins used for linings, while the heavier satin is used for the outer special occasion outfit.

The natural fibers used in previous decades or eras have in many cases become so delicate they can only be stored in a museum setting. The intense ironing, dry cleaning, spot cleaning, and general up-keep of natural fibers like silk and wool are not always as useful in our current setting. Cottons, and linens, have great usage among home seamstresses for quilts and general home décor. However, there are still many ladies who find enormous use in these fabrics for summer skirts and dresses. Meanwhile, the synthetic blends, the many shades of polyester, are utilized with great success because they wash and wear well in many settings from play clothes, to lined suits, to special occasion outfits.

The last, but most popular, classification of fabric is style. What is style? Everyone has a style based on personal likes or dislikes of color, fit, and design. However, the style, of which we are speaking, is the one which categorizes clothing into eras, based on similarities of cut and design, regardless of the personal fit of the individual person. It does help to recall where and when a particular cut was introduced and the history surrounding the design. Therefore, we have some historically famous periods of similar clothing found in the Regency period, the Edwardian period, and the Victorian style, all of which are named after a particular monarch who was deemed the forerunner of fashionable style. In the twentieth century we have less colorful titles - mostly decade numerations of particular clothing, such as the twenties, thirties, forties, etc.

This classification can present a significant problem among ladies and girls. It creates a dating system which stifles creativity to only what is deemed currently fashionable by a select minority. A few of these decades in particular are noted historically by the prominent persons with the latest innovation, regardless of it being proper or not. The '20s were fashionably regulated by Coco Chanel and Jean Patou, the '30s by Elsa Schiaparelli in Europe and Gilbert Adrian through movie actresses, the '40s mainly through government regulations and Hollywood actresses, the '50s through the artistic innovations of Dior, Fath, Givenchy, and popular artists, and the '60s by Saint-Laurent, Courreges, and Mary Quant. The most recent decades have become a hodgepodge to a certain extent, but not all. Everything goes is only allowed for the sexy, extreme, chic, fashionable to current modes, and what is deemed "classic."

The implications are that every ten years to within every ten years there must be funding for a whole new wardrobe to "fit in" with the "new" current modern woman. This can generate vanity, insecurity, and greed. If a girl/woman does not live up to these changes, she is looked down upon as out-of-date and not fit to be in the same social standing as the "in" group. It further creates division and disgust for the older generation, who are viewed as one with their clothing. This mentality has been passed down to our age especially, but not limited, among tweens, teenagers, and young women. (Note: To buy something new occasionally is not the same mentality and can be sincerely enjoyed.) ☺

Now we have been speaking of the extreme; however, this system sadly finds its way into the Catholic minded woman as well. Pope Pius XII said that it is well and good to dress within the time we live. However, he said this once in comparison to the innumerous times he decried the decrepit fashions which kept being introduced at an insidious rate. There are some Catholic women who are afraid to look slightly different from anyone around them either through vanity, pride, or potential ridicule. Others reject everything in the modern age and seek to dress in an age when purity was upheld. Some try to strike a bargain with the world and dress in the world's current idea of conservative, which changes as the wind blows, is a very slippery slope, and eventually leads to corruption. One cannot live in perpetual denial; one will choose one direction or the other ultimately.

Most Catholics are aware of Our Lady of Fatima and her very famous statements and predictions. Of them she states, "The Church has no fashion; Our Lord is always the same." With this idea in mind, it follows then that under Pope Pius XI, he would have had stated, "in order that uniformity of understanding prevail ... we recall that a dress cannot be called decent which is cut deeper than two fingers breadth under the pit of the throat, which does not cover the arms at least to the elbows,* and scarcely reaches a bit beyond the knees. Furthermore, dresses of transparent material are improper." This does not restrict beauty; it directs proper beauty. For all Catholic women, this opens the door to every beautiful design, past, present, and future, that upholds purity and modesty. Our current age encompasses most of the twentieth century in technology and design. We can use a collar introduced from the teens, a sleeve from the forties, a gored skirt from the fifties, etc. All of these are open to us, providing they are done modestly, because we are not of the world. We live in the world and must be a shining light for those who have not found the beauty of purity.

If we are, by chance, ridiculed because through historical dating we may look like another time that the world rejects, we must teach our daughters that those who throw insults do not understand the beauty of purity. We must hold this virtue to a high degree. Virtues are not fearful when done for love of God. When a virtue is practiced or taught badly in fear, resentment will grow and the desire to rebel will come and be manifested with time. This does not mean the virtue should be cast aside, belittled, or ignored as impossible to attain, because of improper circumstances. Instead, it needs to be uplifted, taught, and practiced appropriately all the more in our lives and homes as a beautiful example. Furthermore, we can relish in creativity and beauty within the guides of Holy Mother Church. Historical dating of fabric and clothing is useful as stated, but beware when it is used to demean a lady/girl who looks like another time. If her purity and modesty shine through, this is most important, not the date of her outfit. If someone is poor, but still sews a long cotton skirt, she should be viewed as the great women of old who even in hard times maintained their purity and modesty. Those who prefer current or modern patterns to form modest beauty should also be commended for their talent and foresight to continue good ingenuity in this realm.

The world is crafty; we must be aware. Prudence Glynn, fashion historian, noted, "The most simple way for Society to get away with wearing practically anything, or practically nothing, was to pretend that their fashions were inspired by some great bygone age. Thus when confronted with accusations of indecency they could pretend an innocent hauteur(haughtiness) towards anyone who complained." This is especially true of garments called "classic." Many times, but not all, they are traps towards impurity. The same historian again notes, "Showing a scantily clad woman in a 'classical' role has been a typical trick of Society to dodge conventional or authoritarian ruling."

If you wear a decent blouse with a pair of jeans, it is called "chic." If you wear the same blouse with a skirt, you are immediately rejected as out-of-date. If you wear a long boho skirt with a spaghetti strap camisole, it is "cool." If you wear the same skirt with a real blouse with sleeves, it is rejected as a "prairie" outfit. Speaking of prairie clothes, they were <u>high fashion</u> in the late '70s through the '80s and early '90s, which is roughly ONLY 30 years ago! Another item of interest would be bolero jackets. They appeared in the Regency period(early 1800's) and again in the '30s and '50s. They are very popular right now as well, but no one seems to label them as out-of-date, despite their historical age. It would seem then that charity allows for all outfits that are pure and modest. It allows for continued creativity within a Catholic minded individual who sets their sites on eternity and not on the corruption of worldly decadent fashions.

Our Lady of Good Success said, "<u>Innocence will almost no longer be found in children, nor modesty in women, and in this supreme moment of need of the Church, those who should speak will fall silent</u>." With this in mind, it is strikingly important to raise our daughters and sons, with a love for virtue, especially purity. Pope Pius XII said that modesty is the guardian of purity, and it is especially dear to Our Lord and Our Lady. Young children and especially teenage girls need to understand and be trained from a toddler that their nature is beautiful and must be guarded against worldly influence. This can be done well through personal example and living the faith. By not condemning the women of the world, but condemning their indecent outfits and at the same time explaining how the clothes can be made better to please God first. It can be difficult to separate the woman/girl from the clothes as Professor Lurie explains, "Long before I am near enough to talk to you on the street, in a meeting, or at a party, you announce your sex, age and class to me through what you are wearing-and very possibly give me important information (or misinformation) as to your occupation, origin, personality, opinions, tastes, sexual desires and current mood. I may not be able to put what I observe into words, but I register the information unconsciously; and you simultaneously do the same for me. By the time we meet and converse we have already spoken to each other in an older and more universal tongue." However, they must be separated so that only a healthy rejection of the corrupted garment exists, and not a rejection of the soul that may desperately need help.

Dr. Swigart similarly observed that, "habits, like clothing, are external to us, and a product of our choices. We need to choose them carefully, and change them if necessary; to insure that they accurately reflect who we really are, the things that matter most, and the impressions we want to be remembered by." We need to teach girls to live and work within their own nature and not be jealous of a boy's nature. Each has their own inherent struggles and joys. A girl does not have an inferior nature and needs to understand this and cultivate habits and clothing that reflect a solid understanding of the beauty she possesses. The world will seek to corrupt her through fashion, through amusements, through anything that will make a girl resent herself and desire to be a man. Or it will shift the focus away from eternity and she will want to be desired and liked by men for the wrong reason. Teaching girls to sew creatively and purely, to cook, to plant, to write, to draw, to paint, to play, to be joyful, to pray, to enjoy what God has given her, are all noteworthy and realistic aspirations.

Fiber, fabrics, and clothes are fun, enjoyable, and worthwhile when used properly to maintain purity. Let us always organize the things of this world towards this beloved goal of the saints. As

Reverend George Kelly said so well to parents, "eternal vigilance is the price of sanctity."

My Footnote: (Short sleeves were permitted as a temporary concession, with ecclesiastical approval, because of "impossible market conditions." Hammond, Colleen: Dressing With Dignity TAN Books.).

St. Alphonsus De Liguori's Prayer for Purity

To be said after each of three Hail Mary's morning and night:

"By thy Holy and Immaculate Conception, O Mary, make my body pure and my soul holy. Amen."

26

5. TIDBITS FROM FATHER LAWRENCE G. LOVASIK

Be Affable Always

There are some who are affable and gracious to everyone as long as things go according to their wishes; but if they meet with a contradiction, if an accident, a reproach or even less should trouble the serenity of their soul, all around them must suffer the consequences. They grow dark and cross; very far from keeping up the conversation by their good humor, they answer only monosyllables to those who speak to them. Is this conduct reasonable? Is it Christian?

It is to be regretted that so many people who are very pious are very censorious in their comments upon their neighbors. Piety ought to find expression in kindness to our neighbors as well as in devotion to God. We should remember that the Christ who we serve was kind.

Enthusiasm

It is faith in something, and enthusiasm for something, that makes a life worth looking at. – Oliver Wendell Holmes.

Keep a hobby and ride it with enthusiasm. It will keep you out of mischief, to say the least; it will keep you cheerful. Here as in all things you can apply the *Ad Majorem Dei Gloriam (to the greater glory of God).*

Home is the place where a man should appear at his best. He who is bearish at home and polite only abroad is no true gentleman; indeed, he who cannot be considerate to those of his own household will never really be courteous to strangers. There is no better training for healthy and pleasant intercourse with the outer world than a bright and cheerful demeanor at home. It is in a man's home that his real character is seen; as he appears there, so he is really elsewhere, however skillfully he may for the time conceal his true nature.

<u>Promote Happiness in Your Homes</u>

It would do much in the home if all the members of the family were to be as kind and courteous to one another as they are to guests. The visitor receives bright smiles, pleasant words, constant attention, and the fruits of efforts to please. But the home folks are often cross, rude, selfish, and faultfinding toward one another. Are not our own as worthy of our love and care as is the stranger temporarily within our gates?

A Sunshiny Disposition

There is a charm which compensates so much for the lack of good looks that they are never missed, and when combined with good looks it doubly enhances them. The name of this charm is **a sunshiny disposition.** If things go wrong, as they will go once in a while, does it mend matters to cry over them? Sensible women will say "No," the women who do not know how to control themselves will say: "Yes, it does me good to cry; I feel better after it." There are times when tears must come, but these are beautiful, holy tears. Quite the contrary are the tears shed over selfish, petty annoyances "to relieve nerves." The grandest quality of the human mind is self-control.

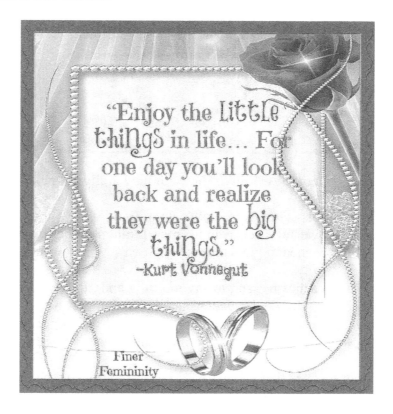

"Enjoy the Little things in life... For one day you'll look back and realize they were the big things."
–Kurt Vonnegut

Finer Femininity

6. YOUR CHILD'S MORAL TRAINING

By Rev. George A. Kelly, The Catholic Family Handbook

In no other aspect of your child's upbringing will your example exert such a powerful force as in his moral training. For your words to your child are meaningless unless your own actions confirm them.

A mother teaches her son to say morning and night prayers, but she says neither. He is only seven years old, but already he questions why prayer is necessary for him but not for adults. One need not be a prophet to realize that he will stop praying as soon as he can.

A father teaches that it is wrong to use the Lord's name in vain; but whenever things go wrong around the house, he spews forth profanity. His son likewise swears at every chance he gets.

A father tells his children that they must respect authority, but he belittles his own employers, criticizes elected officials of the country in the most insulting ways, and makes sneering remarks about priests and his boys' teachers. And he cannot understand why his sons get into trouble for disobeying school regulations.

If you could examine records of families from generation to generation, you would see undisputed proof of the priceless power of example.

In one family, a man now eighty learned from his father's example that men went to church only for baptisms, weddings, and funerals. The man tried to teach his own son to attend Mass as required by Church law, but neglected to do so himself. His son followed his example--not his teaching--and his grandson now also does likewise.

More than a hundred years ago, a merchant made a fortune by cheating townspeople who shopped at his store. His grandson is a "respectable businessman," but he too believes that deception is justifiable if it makes money.

On the other hand, men and women who are long dead but who lived holy lives have left a heritage that lives on in the sanctity of their children's children.

Therefore, if you would help your child to achieve his true purpose--the living of his life in accordance with the will of God so that he may save his soul, and if you would see your good influence continue for untold future generations, provide an example that gives the holy guidance he needs.

7. THE SPIRIT OF THE KITCHEN

By Emilie Barnes, The Spirit of Loveliness

"No matter where I serve my guests, it seems they like my kitchen best."

That little painted plaque in my kitchen is more than just a cute saying for the wall. It's the way I've felt all my life. Wherever I've lived, the kitchen has always seemed to be the place where warmth and love reign.

Family and friends are drawn there like chickens to their roosts. Of all the rooms in our home, the kitchen is the place of comfort, the preferred gathering place for shared conversations and the teamwork of preparing good meals for and with each other.

For me as a young girl, the kitchen was always where I wanted to be - sitting on the countertop as ingredients flew everywhere, tantalizing aromas floated through the air, and meals and memories were created.

After my father died and my mother and I took up quarters in three rooms behind her little dress shop, the kitchen was still the center of warmth.

I remember so many times when Mama welcomed me home with a baked potato, hot cocoa, cinnamon apples, or popovers in winter; popsicles or ice cold lemonade in summer.

All these were expressions of love, and they all came from the kitchen.

The Heart of the Home

Even today, the kitchen feels like the heart of home to me. The smell of garlic and onions being sautéed in butter draws me to the kitchen. Coffee, brewing fresh in the pot, lifts and warms my heart.

I love to bend over a bubbling pot of soup or gaze out the window while quietly bringing order to my countertops. And I love to smile at all the photographs of family and friends that smile back at me from the refrigerator door.

My kitchen is filled with heart. My pots hang on hooks above the stove the way my dad's pots did in his commercial kitchens. Plants line the windowsill, including a few pots of herbs to snip when needed. A crock holds my whips, wooden spoons, and spatulas in a space-saving and attractive bouquet. A collection of special plaques and pictures from friends and family decorates my "love wall" at one end of the room.

Above all, make your kitchen a room you enjoy and feel good in.

8. MAKING THE MOST OF MEALTIME

By Emilie Barnes, The Spirit of Loveliness

Much of our lifetime is spent in a food related atmosphere. If you are a woman forty-five years or older, you've already spent over fifty thousand hours in the kitchen and eaten over fifty thousand meals!

Since we spend so much of our lives eating, preparing to eat, and cleaning up after ourselves, shouldn't we put some effort and attention into making mealtimes some of the most pleasurable and memorable parts of our lives?

What makes a memorable meal?

The recipe for such a time involves four ingredients:

The Setting

The attractive way you set the table sets the tone for a meal and can convey affection, warmth, and caring. The simple way the napkin is fluffed up in the glass, folded to make a flower, or creatively arranged in a napkin ring can speak your love and concern. The garnish of parsley on the platter of roast chicken or a wedge of lemon in the glass of water say, "I care enough to do the little bit it takes to be above average." A floral sheet made into a unique tablecloth with matching napkins can be creative and inexpensive.

Centerpieces are great for establishing a mood. But a centerpiece can be so much more than a case of chrysanthemums plopped in the middle of a table. An autumn table lined down the middle with apples, pears, grapes, winter squash and Indian corn smiles a beautiful welcome. A swatch of pine twinkling with tiny white lights and festive with tiny wooden toys sets a Christmassy mood. Individual vases holding single blooms can freshen up individual place settings. And candles are always wonderful. Use them liberally to create the spirit of warmth at mealtime.

The Food

Obviously, food takes the starring role at any meal. The warm, caring spirit of the kitchen extends to providing food that is both delicious and healthful. The old adage, "You are what you eat" is really true. When we eat right, we look better and feel better. Our mental and physical health improves. We have more energy and endurance to carry out the task of loving others.

Given the fact that healthy eating is so important, isn't it great that healthy meals can also taste wonderful? Many of the most healthy foods - fruits and vegetables, especially - are also the most pleasing to the eye. Learning to eat a wholesome variety of foods can be a delicious adventure that adds another exciting dimension to the spirit of the kitchen.

When you are planning your meals, doing your shopping, or just puttering in the kitchen, don't forget to take your nose into account! Aromas are memory triggers; they invoke recollections of the past happiness. You can build those kinds of memories through the wonderful aromas of the kitchen. The smell of garlic, curry, cinnamon, fresh bread, or coffee can combine with wonderful tastes and warm feelings to instill the spirit of the kitchen deep in the souls of your family, your guests, and you.

The Fellowship

Mealtime is traditionally a time for family and guests to gather and share their lives. But hectic schedules make home-made family meals a thing of the past for many families. It's worth the effort to buck this trend and share a family meal. Turn off the TV, unplug the phone and sit down together for a time of fellowship and food.

Expect some resistance if your family is out of practice at fellowship. You might want to stimulate conversation with some questions such as "What is the best thing that happened to you today?" Be prepared to share, and be prepared to listen.

Mealtime is not the only opportunity for "kitchen style" fellowship, of course. Some of my most reassured conversations have happened while two of us were cooking or cleaning up together. Afterschool snacks, afternoon tea, and late-night popcorn sessions all provide safe, comfortable opportunities for sharing lives as well as sharing the spirit of the kitchen.

Some of the richest kind of kitchen fellowship comes when we extend the spirit of the kitchen to those outside our homes and families. Surely this is part of what Jesus meant when he said, "I was hungry and you fed me." People who volunteer to cook at a soup kitchen, deliver meals on wheels, or help with an emergency food drive discover that they are richly blessed by the opportunity to share the spirit of the kitchen with someone in need.

A Peaceful Ambience

"Better a dry crust with peace and quiet than a house full of feasting with strife" (Proverbs 17:1). That was true in Solomon's day, and it's especially true in today's high-stress, stomach-churning society. Peaceful mealtimes aid both the digestion and the disposition; they are well worth the effort they take.

How can mealtimes be more related? Careful panning helps, so that dishes are ready at the same time and you don't have to keep running to the kitchen. Food should be simple and wholesome and tailored to the needs of family and guests. (Serving spicy or difficult-to-handle food to small children, for example, just invites tension and frustration.)

Conversation can be lively and even provocative, but it's good to postpone weighty or emotional issues for another time. Beautiful, soothing music in the background helps everyone to calm down and enjoy the meal.

Perhaps the most meaningful and effective way to bring an air of peace and grace to mealtime is to make a habit of inciting God to be present. Even a mumbled and hurried "Bless us O Lord…" helps turn our hearts in the direction of gratitude and peace. But how much better to really stop, take a quiet moment, and ask the Lord's blessing on the meal and those gathered around the table.

May these walls be filled with laughter, MAY IT REACH FROM FLOOR TO RAFTER. *May the roof keep out the rain,* MAY SUNSHINE WARM EACH WINDOWPANE. *And may the door be open wide* TO LET THE GOOD LORD'S LOVE INSIDE. -Irish Blessing

9. LUKEWARMNESS?
Searching For and Maintaining Peace
by Father Jacques Philippe

Don't Let Your Apparent Lukewarmness Upset You

Don't allow yourself to become disheartened or discouraged if it appears that you are making no progress, if you are fainthearted and lukewarm, if you should see that you are still subject to natural affections, thoughts of pride and sad feelings.

Simply strive to forget all these things and turn your mind toward God, standing before Him in the quiet and continuous desire that He make of you and in you His holy pleasure.

Aim only at forgetting yourself and at walking before Him in the midst of your poverty, without ever looking at yourself...As long as you are concerned with the capriciousness of nature, you will be busy with yourself and, as long as you are busy with yourself, you will not make much progress on the way to perfection.

These capricious movements will stop only when you hold them in contempt and forget them. Besides, I assure you that they are of no importance nor of any consequence, don't pay any attention to them, only look at God and this with a pure and simple faith.

Don't Worry About Your Falls

Always forget the past and never worry about your falls, many as they may be. So long as you get back on your feet, no harm will have been done; whereas, a great deal of harm will occur if you lose heart of if you berate yourself too much for your failures.

Do everything with the greatest possible calm and serenity and out of the greatest, purest and holiest love of Jesus and Mary.

Patience

One of the principal obstacles one encounters on the way to perfection is the precipitous and impatient desire to progress and to possess those virtues that we feel we don't have.

On the contrary, the true means of solidly advancing, and with giant steps, is to be patient and to calm and pacify these anxieties....Don't get ahead of your guide for fear of getting lost and straying from the path that He indicates, because if you do, instead of arriving safe and sound, you will fall into a pit.

Your guide is the Holy Spirit. By your struggles and worries, by your anxiety and haste, you overtake Him with the pretense of moving more quickly.

And then what happens? You stray from the path and find yourself on terrain that is harder and rougher and, far from advancing, you go backwards; at a minimum, you waste your time.

Let the Spirit of God Act

When it pleased God to create the universe, He worked with nothing, and look at the beautiful things He made! In the same way, if He wants to work in us to accomplish things infinitely beyond all the natural beauties which came from His hands, He doesn't need our becoming so agitated to help Him...

Rather, let Him work by Himself; He likes to work with nothingness. Let us stay peacefully and quietly before Him and simply follow the changes that He produces....

Let us then keep our souls at peace and our spiritual forces at rest before Him, while awaiting every motion and sign of life from Him alone.

And let us endeavor not to move, will or live, except in God and through the Spirit of God. It is necessary to forget oneself and continually direct one's soul toward God and leave it calmly and peacefully before Him.

Why, then, Has He chosen us, knowing that we can do nothing, if not to demonstrate, with evidence, that it is He Who will do the work and not we?

-Venerable François-Marie-Paul Libermann

10. HOSPITALITY

from True Womanhood

Rev. Bernard O'Reilly, L.D., 1893

Let each one inquire in the Church for the poor and the stranger; and when he meets them, let him invite them to his house; for with the poor man Christ will enter it. He who entertains a stranger, entertains Christ. The glory of a Christian is to receive strangers and pilgrims, and to have at his table the poor, the widow and the orphan. ST. EPHBEM, De Amore Pauperum.

THE Christian religion, besides inheriting all the divine legislation of preceding ages, and consecrating all that was ennobling and purifying in public and private life, perfected every virtue practiced by Jew and Gentile by assigning to each a supernatural motive and by assisting the weakness of nature with most powerful graces.

Doubtless in the most ancient times, men, wherever they chanced to live, were not altogether unmindful of their being sprung from the same parents, and the first impulse of nature urged them to open their house to the stranger as to a brother, one who was their own flesh and blood.

In the patriarchal ages we find a higher motive superadded to that of common brotherhood: that to receive the stranger, was to discharge a debt due to God Himself; that to shut him out was, possibly, to close one's door against the Deity in disguise.

Abraham and his nephew Lot gave hospitality to angels disguised in human form, and were rewarded, the former by the birth of Isaac, the latter by being saved with his family from the terrible destruction in which Sodom and the neighboring cities were involved.

Not dissimilar was the reward divinely granted to the poor pagan widow of Sarephta who harbored and fed the famished and fugitive prophet Elias, and to the wealthy lady of Sunam who sheltered Elisseus. Their generous hospitality was rewarded by the restoring to life of the only son of each.

But in the gospel, Martha and Mary made their home the resting-place of the Incarnate God, and their hospitality was accompanied by a public and unhesitating confession of their Guest's divinity, and that, too, at a time when He was most opposed and persecuted by the leading men of the nation.

Not only were they, also, rewarded by the restoration to life of their dead brother, but they had the further recompense of becoming the apostles of the Divine Master.

This was, moreover, the return made by Him to his Mother's cousin, Mary Salome, mother of St. James the Elder and St. John the Apostle, for the hospitality so generously bestowed on Mary, after the breaking up of her own home at Nazareth.

The same may be said of that other Mary, the sister of the apostle St. Barnabas, and the mother of another apostle, John-Mark. It is the common tradition that her house was that in which our Lord celebrated the Last Supper, in which the Blessed Virgin found a refuge during the interval between the Crucifixion and the

Resurrection, and in which the apostles and disciples were wont to assemble till the Holy Ghost came down on them.

Certain it is that there the faithful were wont to meet with Peter and the other apostles till after the martyrdom of St. Stephen and St. James, the imprisonment and miraculous liberation of St. Peter, and the visit made to him by St. Paul after the latter's conversion.

Her home was the common home of the infant church of Jerusalem, and, as tradition affirms, the first Christian church in that city. This generous mother's hospitality was rewarded by seeing both her brother and her son called to the glorious labors and perils of the apostleship.

Thenceforward, the bestowing hospitality was for the mistress of a Christian household to receive Christ himself, the God of Charity, in the person of every guest who crossed her threshold, be he rich or poor, kinsman or stranger, friend or foe, sick or loathsome, the holiest of men or the most abandoned of sinners.

"Hospitality is not to CHANGE PEOPLE, but to offer them space where CHANGE CAN TAKE PLACE." –Henri J.M. Noewen

"Love is a mutual SELF-GIVING that ends in SELF-RECOVERY." –Archbishop Fulton J. Sheen

11 . THE ROSARY AND THE BARGAIN

By Joseph A. Breig, 1956

When I get to heaven - as I trust I shall - something very embarrassing is bound to happen. As sure as shooting; somebody who has known me rather too well for comfort on this earth is going to come up to me and say, in a loud voice enough for everybody to hear, "How in the world did you get in here?"

I am not going to answer in words. I am simply going to pull a rosary out of my pocket and dangle it in front of my questioner. That will be my reply; and it will be perfectly true. It will also be true for my family, which I have every reason to hope will be there with me. We will all pull our rosaries out of our pockets and wave them.

I think that we will wave them for all eternity; or at least wear them around our necks for everybody to see. It will save a lot of explaining, and it will give credit where credit is due.

I am not humble enough for public confession of my sins: besides, it would be scandalous; and the readers would be writing to the editor denouncing him for printing such shocking stuff.

I will simply say this: there is a period of my life that I want to forget; and I would still be in it if it weren't for the rosary.

The rosary is the rope by which I climbed hand over hand out of the pit into which I had fallen.

I started climbing out after I discovered one basic rule for any kind of success in life. The way to get something done is to do it. I will never forget how that realization suddenly popped into my head and transformed me.

Ever since then, I have been getting things done, simply by doing them. And the thing that taught me that lesson was the rosary. I do not remember how or why or when I started saying the rosary daily. But I do remember that doing it was the hardest thing I ever did in my life.

When people say to me now that they just can't seem to get at it, I chuckle. They're telling me! They complain about the irregularity of their lives, about visitors dropping in, and whatnot. And I chuckle again.

When I started saying the daily rosary, I was a reporter for a Hearst newspaper in the big city. It was not in the least unusual for me to be out on a story half the night, or three-quarters of the night, or all night.

At any moment during the day, the city editor might answer the telephone, look across the desk at me, and order me to high-ball by automobile, or train or other conveyance to some city or town or crossroads 100, 500, 1000 miles distant.

At any hour of the night, I might be awakened by the telephone and told to dash into the office, or dash somewhere else. As for social and other affairs, I had more than my share of them. But I had discovered that the way to get something done is to do it. I had learned that the way to get the rosary said is to say it. And I said it - and I don't think anybody ever said it harder.

Meditation? It came as naturally to me as eating glass or swallowing swords. Praying? It was hard, sweaty, ditch-digging heavy labor for me. I was going it alone then; and the going was all uphill. It was all mountain climbing.

More than once, I awoke in the wee hours of the night, still on my knees, with the upper half of my body sprawled over the bed, and the rosary still clutched in my fingers at the second or third decade. But the way to get something done was to do it; and I wouldn't allow myself to crawl into bed until the rosary was finished.

I tell all this only in order that the reader may know that I am not one to whom prayer came easily. You say that it is hard for you; I answer that it was hard for me.

Then suddenly, somewhere along the line, I met Father Patrick Peyton, and discovered an additional rule for success. I discovered that whereas it was exceedingly difficult for me to say the rosary alone, it was as easy as rolling off a log to say it with my family.

We were one of the early families in Father Peyton's Family Rosary Crusade; and what he gave to us when he talked us into it, we wouldn't trade today for all the Fords and Lincolns in Henry Ford's factory for the next thousand years.

I state a simple fact; and you needn't take it just from me. Ask my wife. Ask the children. Ask the neighbors. Ask our visitors. They'll all tell you the same thing: that ever since we started the daily family Rosary, and kept it up, our house has been one of the happiest and healthiest homes in the world.

To use a popular jive expression, the place simply jumps with joy. And there were times when it didn't. There were a great many times when it didn't. There was a time when the doctor told us we might as well make up our minds to sell our home for whatever we could get and go to Florida, with or without a job, if we didn't want to see our children dying one by one before our eyes.

He said they simply couldn't stand the climate in which we were living; and they'd be better off living on bananas under a tree in the south than suffering what they were suffering in the north.

The rosary changed all that; and today our youngsters, every one of them, can whip their weight in wildcats; and would do it at the drop of a hat if there were any Wildcats in sight.

But that is the least of the blessings that have come to us from the family Rosary. I remember vividly my first conversation with Father Peyton, long before he became world famous as the originator of the family hour on the radio, in which the greatest stars of Broadway and Hollywood donate their talents to popularize the slogan, "The family that prays together, stays together."

Father Peyton, knitting his brows in the way he has, and speaking in that wonderful Irish brogue which I won't try to reproduce, told me that, when he was first ordained, he planned to start a crusade for daily mass, communion and the rosary.

The longer he prayed and puzzled over it, the more he became convinced that if he asked for everything at first, he'd get nothing; whereas if he could get people to say the rosary, the rosary would lead them to the other things.

Today I can testify that, in our case at least, he was perfectly right. We have learned that the rosary, if you will just say it, takes care of the full spiritual development of the family.

I recall that, when we started it, the children got very tired and restless while kneeling, especially at bedtime. Soon my wife, with the wisdom that God gives to mothers, told the youngsters to sit for the rosary.

Today, the two who are in grade school go to mass and communion daily, carrying their breakfast with him, or buying donuts and milk in the school basement. The rosary drew them naturally and inevitably to mass.

My wife and I often tell friends that someday we are going to write a book entitled "how to rear children." It Is going to have 300 pages, and every page will have three words – and three words only – printed on it. "Let them alone."

But of course there will have to be a preface: "Teach them to pray... And then let them alone."

In spiritual as in all other affairs, we have learned that children need very little preaching to. They ought not to be analyzed and psychoanalyzed and cross-examined and made to toe Chalk Lines.

What they need is prayer and good example – and the rest takes care of itself. I would say this – that by far the easiest and least troublesome way of rearing a family of which you can be proud is to institute the family rosary in your home, and keep it up.

It eliminates almost entirely the need for discipline, because it creates such harmony and such family love that the children discipline themselves. It knits the family together with bonds 10,000 times stronger than any that can be forged by merely natural means.

I think that I've heard all the objections to the family rosary. Fully half the fathers and mothers who have talked with me about it have shrugged their shoulders helplessly and said that there simply doesn't seem to be any time of the day when all the members of the family can be brought together in prayer.

The answer to that, of course, is exceedingly simple. If you can't get all the members of the family together, say the rosary with the members who are present.

Sooner or later, something will happen to make it possible for the others to join in.

The rosary is like that. Give it a chance, and it'll take care of the problems. The Mother of God can have whatever she wants from her divine Son; and one of the things she wants is Rosary Families.

Mothers have said to me that the smaller members of the family won't behave during the rosary. What of it? The smaller members of our family won't behave either.

Between them, our two-year-old Jimmy and eight month old Regina put on something resembling a three ring circus while we are saying the rosary. We don't interfere. It's our business to say to say the rosary; it's theirs to have a circus. God made them that way; and if He doesn't mind, why should we? We pray above and between their shouts and gurgles, and it works out very well.

I have also heard people say that the antics of the smaller children interfere with their meditations. They interfered with mine, too, until I learned to include the youngsters in the meditation.

Now, while saying the Joyful Mysteries, I look at Regina, cooing and bouncing in her crib, and I think, "Why, Christ was just like that once! He cooed and gurgled too, and waved his arms, and kicked his legs, and rolled over on his stomach, then worked like a Trojan to get turned to his back again."

Or if the baby is sitting on her mother's lap, I look at them and realize that the Christ Child sat in Mary's lap too, and clutched at her garments, and tried to pull Himself upright, and swung His hands at her face, and laughed when she smiled at Him.

I think of the fact that He, too, had to be fed; that although He held the universe in the palm of His hand and kept the planets on their courses, He depended on his mother for everything.

Perhaps we are saying the Sorrowful Mysteries. If so, sometimes I look at Jimmy and think how I would feel if he were crucified in front of my eyes. Then I know something about what Mary felt.

I know something, too, about the infinite love of God which caused Him to send His only Son to die for us.

Could I send one of my sons to die in agony for someone who had insulted me? I think of that; and then I am better able to thank God for the redemption.

If we are saying the Glorious Mysteries, I consider often what a moment it will be when all the family rises from the grave and is reunited, nevermore to be parted; when we are all together to stay together, in perfect happiness, forever.

If the happy family is a thing of rollicking joy - and it is - then what must a perfectly happy family in heaven be like! It is very well worth looking forward to. It is very well worth the trouble of saying the daily rosary.

Ten or fifteen minutes a day is what it takes; and eternity is what it purchases. I wasn't born yesterday; and I'm not passing up a bargain like that.

"The Rosary is the Weapon of our Times." – Padre Pio

"Give me an army saying the Rosary and I will conquer the world."
- Blessed Pope Pius IX

WWW.STPETERSLIST.COM

REAL MEN PRAY THE ROSARY

12 .LOSING OUR LIFE

J.R. Miller

"Measure thy life by loss instead of gain;
Not by the wine drunk, but the wine poured forth;
For love's strength standeth in love's sacrifice,
And whoso suffers most hath most to give."
--The Disciples.

According to our Lord's teaching, we can make the most of our life by losing it. He says that losing the life for his sake is saving it. There is a lower self that must be trampled down and trampled to death by the higher self. The alabaster vase must be broken, that the ointment may flow out to fill the house. The grapes must be crushed, that there may be wine to drink. The wheat must be bruised, before it can become bread to feed hunger.

It is so in life. Whole, unbruised, unbroken men are of but little use. True living is really a succession of battles, in which the better triumphs over the worse, the spirit over the flesh. Until we cease to live for self, we have not begun to live at all.

We can never become truly useful and helpful to others until we have learned this lesson. One may live for self and yet do many pleasant things for others; but one's life can never become the great blessing to the world it was meant to be until the law of self-sacrifice has become its heart principle.

A great oak stands in the forest. It is beautiful in its majesty; it is ornamental; it casts a pleasant shade. Under its branches the children play; among its boughs the birds sing. One day the woodman comes with his axe, and the tree quivers in all its branches, under his sturdy blows. "I am being destroyed," it cries. So it seems, as the great tree crashes down to the ground. And the children are sad because they can play no more beneath the broad branches; the birds grieve because they can no more nest and sing amid the summer foliage.

But let us follow the tree's history. It is cut into boards, and built into a beautiful cottage, where human hearts find their happy nest. Or it is used in making a great organ which leads the worship of a congregation. The losing of its life was the saving of it. It died that it might become deeply, truly useful.

The plates, cups, dishes, and vases which we use in our homes and on our tables, once lay as common clay in the earth, quiet and restful, but in no way doing good, serving man. Then came men with picks, and the clay was rudely torn out and plunged into a mortar and beaten and ground in a mill, then pressed, and then put into a furnace, and burned and burned, at last coming forth in beauty, and beginning its history of usefulness. It was apparently destroyed that it might begin to be of service.

These are simple illustrations of the law which applies also in human life. We must die to be useful--to be truly a blessing. Our Lord put this truth in a little parable, when He said that the seed must fall into the earth and die that it may bear fruit. Christ's own cross is the highest illustration of this.

His friends said he wasted his precious life; but was that life wasted when Jesus was crucified?

George MacDonald in one of his little poems, with deep spiritual insight, presents this truth of the blessed gain of Christ's life through his sacrifice and death:--

"For three and thirty years, a living seed,
A lonely germ, dropt on our waste world's side,
Thy death and rising, thou didst calmly bide;
Sore compassed by many a clinging weed
Sprung from the fallow soil of evil and need;
Hither and thither tossed, by friends denied;
Pitied of goodness dull, and scorned of pride;
Until at length was done the awful deed,
And thou didst lie outworn in stony bower--
Three days asleep--oh, slumber godlike, brief,
For Man of sorrows and acquaint with grief,
Heaven's seed, Thou diedst, that out of thee might tower
Aloft, with rooted stem and shadowy leaf
Of all Humanity the crimson flower."

"It was in a mine in England. There had been a fearful explosion, and the men came rushing up from the lower level, right into the danger of the deathly afterblast; when the only chance of safety was in another shaft. And one man knew this and stood there in the dangerous passage, warning the men. When urged to go himself the safe way, he said, "No; someone must stay here to guide the others." Is there any heroism of this world's life finer than that?

It was at Fredericksburg, after a bloody battle. Hundreds of Union soldiers lay wounded on the field. All night and all next day the space was swept by artillery from both armies; and no one could venture to the sufferers' relief. All that time, too, there went up from the field agonizing cries for water, but there was no response save the roar of the guns. At length, however, one brave fellow behind the ramparts, a Southern soldier, felt that he could endure these piteous cries no longer. His compassion rose superior to his love of life.

"General," said Richard Kirkland to his commander, "I can't stand this.
Those poor souls out there have been praying for water all night and all day, and it is more than I can bear. I ask permission to carry them water."

The general assured him that it would be instant death for him to appear upon the field, but he begged so earnestly that the officer, admiring his noble devotion to humanity, could not refuse his request.

Provided with a supply of water, the brave soldier stepped over the wall and went on his Christ-like errand. From both sides wondering eyes looked on as he knelt by the nearest sufferer, and gently raising his head, held the cooling cup to his parched lips. At once the Union soldiers understood what the soldier in gray was doing for their own wounded comrades, and not a shot was fired. For an hour and a half he continued his work, giving drink to the thirsty, straightening cramped and mangled limbs, pillowing men's heads on their knapsacks, and spreading blankets and army coats over them, tenderly as a mother would cover her child; and all the while, until this angel-ministry was finished, the fusillade of death was hushed.

Did this soldier not risk everything to give to others?

Again we must admire the heroism that led this brave soldier in gray so utterly to forget himself for the sake of doing a deed of mercy to his enemies. There is more grandeur in five minutes of such self-renunciation than in a whole lifetime of self-interest and self-seeking. There is something Christly in it. How poor, paltry, and mean, alongside the records of such deeds, appear men's selfish strivings, self-interests' boldest venturing!

We must get the same spirit in us if we would become in any large and true sense a blessing to the world. We must die to live. We must lose our life to save it. We must lay self on the altar to be consumed in the fire of love, in order to glorify God and do good to men. Our work may be fair, even though mingled with self; but it is only when self is sacrificed, burned on the altar of consecration, consumed in the hot flames of love, that our work becomes really our best, a fit offering to be made to our King.

We must not fear that in such sacrifice, such renunciation and annihilation of self, we shall lose ourselves. God will remember every deed of love, every forgetting of self, every emptying out of life.
Though we work in obscurest places, where no human tongue shall ever voice our praise, still there is a record kept, and some day rich and glorious reward will be given. Is not God's praise better than man's?

"Ungathered beauties of a bounteous earth,
Wild flowers which grow on mountain-paths untrod.
White water-lilies looking up to God
From solitary tarns--and human worth
Doing meek duty that no glory gains,
Heroic souls in secret places sown,
To live, to suffer, and to die unknown--
Are not that loveliness and all these pains
Wasted? Alas, then does it not suffice
That God is on the mountain, by the lake,
And in each simple duty, for whose sake
His children give their very blood as price?
The Father sees. If this does not repay,
What else? For plucked flowers fade and praises slay."

Mary's ointment was wasted when she broke the vase and poured it upon her Lord. Yes; but suppose she had left the ointment in the unbroken vase? What remembrance would it then have had? Would there have been any mention of it on the Gospel pages? Would her deed of careful keeping have been told over all the world? She broke the vase and poured it out, lost it, sacrificed it, and now the perfume fills all the earth. We may keep our life if we will, carefully preserving it from waste; but we shall have no reward, no honor from it, at the last.

But if we empty it out in loving service, we shall make it a lasting blessing to the world, and we shall be remembered forever.

Some may say that those missionaries who go out in the field only to be martyred have wasted their lives....buried far from home without anyone to see their courage and their love. But were their lives wasted?

What about those sacrificing men and women who lay down their lives in service of Our Lord in the religious life. Are their lives wasted as they labor out of love in Christ's Church?
No, these men and women are the inspirations to mankind. Their influence is everywhere touching lives far and wide.

What about women who lay down their lives for their families? They live the everyday toil, unrewarded and unnoticed. Their lives speak of sweetness and their gentle hearts do work that will touch the world in generations to come.
These men and women die so they may live.

We must do the same. In order to be a blessing to this world we must be willing to lose our life----to sacrifice ourselves, give up our own way, our comforts, maybe one day even our life. It is this way...the way of "losing oneself in Christ" that is the road to happiness and to salvation.

"The thought of the importance of your position as a Catholic mother should be a *SOURCE OF JOY TO YOU.*
But your **battle will often be hard** and your ***SPIRITUAL CONSOLATIONS FEW.***
It is good sometimes to know that although you have sacrificed many of the things modern 'emancipated' women value so highly, your humble position is still the PROUDEST IN SOCIETY.

You are the ***POSSESSOR OF THE HAND*** that ROCKS THE CRADLE AND RULES THE WORLD.

You are to be the **comforter,** the **unchanging inspiration,** and the **educator of souls.**"

- Fr. Lovasik

13. IDEALIZING FATHER – FATHER LEO KINSELLA, 1950'S

From The Wife Desired

A young man unconsciously looks for the qualities of his mother in his wife. Foolishly he may give expression to comparisons. We are all familiar with the refrain, "Mother made the best apple pie ever eaten." It may be strange, but seldom do these encomiums paid to mother produce in the wife a warm glow of affection for her husband. On the other hand, the young wife is inclined to expect her husband to mirror her father, especially if he was a real man. Her father did things this or that way.

The ideal wife guards against this usual idealization of her father. Her husband is another man. There are other ways of doing things beside the way father did them. Father is a fine man. Yet it would be a dull world if all men were similar to him. The sensible wife does not try to mold her husband after him. She is not inspiring her husband to develop his own abilities and personality by so doing.

Mr. X did not seem to be the type of man who drank to excess to escape reality. He seemed to be more of a social drinker. His reality appeared to be a very pleasant one from which no one would want to escape. He enjoyed many blessings. His wife was an attractive woman. They had several exceptionally beautiful daughters whom they both took great pleasure in displaying on many social occasions. Although his salary was not fabulous, it was considerably above average and ran into five figures. They made a handsome couple as they sat in their box at the race track.

Their daughters added to the picture. They surely were the envy of the crowd. Yet all was not well. In fact, his wife was on the verge of calling it quits. She never knew when he would come home or in what condition.

He had no complaints against his wife and wanted to keep the marriage. He promised reform, willingly admitting that he had been giving her a rather hard time. His position was of the type which readily could be the occasion of an excessive amount of social drinking. He had let it get out of hand, was going to put a stop to it, and would quit completely if necessary.

Several months went by, and then the word came from the wife that his reform was short lived. Several weeks after they had been down to the Chancery he was back to his heavy drinking.

After getting more familiar with the couple, I began to be a little suspicious that his reason for drinking lay with her. It is not often that an excessive drinker has not one single complaint against his wife. Was she such an ideal wife that even her half-drunk husband could find no fault in her? Or was he hiding something which stung him deep down inside? In all outward appearances he had been a very successful man. He was regarded in a wide circle of friends and acquaintances as a polished man about town. Was someone missing in this group of admirers?

From a reliable source, not usually available, the information came to me that he never had her esteem, admiration and inspiration. She had a rugged, masterful sort of father, a real two-fisted he-man. She worshiped him as a child and young woman. As a young wife she compared him with her husband and found her husband wanting. She really never gave herself completely to her husband.

Yes, outwardly she did. She smiled sweetly at him. She was faithful and dutiful in all the varied activities of married life. But that inner spark was missing, and he knew it. He was too proud to admit, probably even to himself, that he had failed to win her full love, the kind of love that goes overboard and blindly says, "You are the best there is."

Perhaps this woman had not matured sufficiently. She was still the little girl at her father's knee. She did not have to think any the less of her father because she had married. By analyzing her husband, by breaking him up into the parts of a jigsaw puzzle and being unable to fit him into the pattern of her father, she underestimated him. No two people are alike. Suppose that she had attempted to fit her father into the character and pattern of her husband. They still would not have dovetailed. That would not have made father necessarily any less a man, only a different man.

To the casual observer this woman would seem to be an ideal wife. Yet she had failed her husband in the most important role a wife must play in marriage. Like any husband this man wanted her and needed her for his inspiration, but she would not or could not deliver the goods. What a man required most from his wife was lacking. So many wives seem to have no realization of what their husbands have a right to expect first from them, and not getting it, little else matters.

He saw himself not measuring up to her standards. He looked into the mirror of her eyes and saw himself deflated. The eyes of a wife are a man's mirror. When he looks into them and sees a veritable giant on wheels, it is like strong wine. He feels like a giant ready to take the world by the tail and swing it. When he sees a little dwarf in her eyes, he begins to feel like one and to act like one. He may put on a big show with lots of bluster. Lacking conviction from her he may go to all extremes to convince himself that he is a "big shot." He tries hard to magnify the puny vision of himself. With all sorts of maneuvers, bragging, condemnation and belittling of others, and drinking he strives to grow in stature in her eyes. The more frantic become these efforts, the more he sees his image shrinking in the mirror of her eyes.

Of course, there are plenty of cases where the wife is only half to blame. Ideal wives have a way of going with ideal husbands. A man has no business marrying a woman unless he is in love with her, unless she had become the most beautiful thing in life to him. If during the years of their marriage he continues to look into her eyes and tell her of this beauty to him she will grow more beautiful for him. Too many husbands do not know that a woman must be told that she is beautiful in order to be beautiful. A wife who is being told that she is most beautiful will glow with love for her husband. He will see in her eyes this love for him. Then she will be looking back at him through rose colored glasses. She sees nothing but good in him. The mirror is highly polished and sparkling, and he fills it. He has everything she can give now, and the greatest of her gifts is the inspiration a man needs from his wife to be a husband and a man.

I have no recollection of a single broken marriage wherein the wife was primarily to blame and at the same time an inspiration to her husband. Failure and inspiration do not mix well. The ability to inspire her husband is the wife's best guarantee of success in marriage. Only if she fails to inspire need she be fearful for their love and the future of their marriage. How can a wife miss if she has her man jumping up and down beside himself in excitement of effort to fill those big blue eyes of his wife? All right, make them green. They are still the most beautiful eyes in the world to him, because he sees himself in them. Men are much vainer than any woman ever dreamed of being.

Very few inspirational wives fail in marriage through their own fault. It is possible for a wife to give all desired in the way of inspiration and receive no response. Admittedly, no wife, be she so perfect in this respect, can inspire a cabbage. But be it known to all women that few mortal males can resist inspiration. They thrive on it. They are "dead ducks" when women look down the sights of their not too secret weapon, their inspiration.

Frequently single young ladies raise an objection: "How can I inspire, show appreciation, and make the young man with whom I am going think that he is the greatest man in the world to me? He already leans over backward in trying to make me think he is the answer to every maiden's prayer. He is already so conceited I shudder to think of blowing him up any more. I often wonder if he never wears a hat because he can find none to fit his head." Married women seldom ask a question like this. Is it because of their experience they sense that inspiration does not make a husband conceited?

The answer to this objection already has been given to discerning readers, but, because it is commonly heard, an explicit reply should be made. Conceit is usually symptomatic of an inferiority complex. All the manifold gyrations of a conceited man, his bragging, his puffing and huffing. his belittling of others, all his noise and bluster, are efforts to convince the world of something of which he himself is not convinced, namely, that he is a man. If he were sure of himself, he would not be worrying his head about whether or not the rest of men are sure of him.

The inspiration of a wife is the best tonic in the world against a husband's conceit. He has confidence from her as well as from his own consciousness of himself. He is not selling himself short because he knows that the best there is in the world is long on him. Nor does the inspired husband sit back in self-satisfaction. He is charged into action to measure up to the esteem of the one most precious to him. He feels unworthy of her but is not thereby depressed. He thrills to the excitement of planning to do big things for her. Nothing will be too good for his love. To preserve her as she is he would wrap her in cellophane or fine spun gold. What obstacle could thwart him in keeping her lovely and happy?

Can a husband be conceited who loses himself so completely in such a consuming blaze of love for his wife? The conceited man is forever concerned with himself; the inspired man is forever concerned with the source of his inspiration.

So take it from me, ladies, inspiration is your love potion. Men wander through the cold world seeking the warm eyes of inspiration like a thirsting deer panting after fountains of water. Not having it, they are lost souls. On finding it, they leap for joy, and the very mountains break forth into singing. So, be kind, ladies, lest men die of hunger and thirst. Give hope and encouragement to carry on. It is so easy for you; just be as God made you, His loveliest of creatures.

After speaking on this absorbing topic of inspiration, I have often been asked how a woman can inspire her husband. The question at first was disconcerting after having spent fifteen or twenty minutes on the subject. But I suppose there is no way to humility except down the road of humiliations. The only answer I have ever given to this query is as follows: God has not given to me but to you, ladies, the ability to inspire. You are asking me how to inspire? To you have gone God's gifts. Within your being you hold from Him the power of life and death for the poor creatures of the weaker sex. With inspiration from you men vibrate with life. Wanting it, they go through the motion of living.

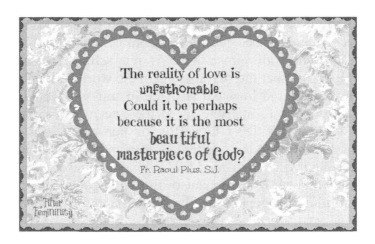

The reality of love is unfathomable. Could it be perhaps because it is the most beautiful masterpiece of God?

Fr. Raoul Plus. S.J.

14. QUESTIONS YOUNG PEOPLE ASK BEFORE MARRIAGE

FR. DONALD MILLER, C.SS.R, 1950'S

Problem:

Is love necessary for a happy marriage?

Solution:

It depends on what you mean by "love". I might add that it also depends on what you mean by marriage, but we shall take for granted that you mean what the Lord meant, viz., an indissoluble sacramental partnership between a man and a woman who pledge themselves to help each other toward happiness on earth and in heaven, and to beget and rear children for the kingdom of God.

What do you mean by "love"? Do you mean that violent feeling of attraction, that all-suffering sense of helpless infatuation, that overpowering "can't-think-of-anything-else" emotion, which the pulps, true story magazines and mashy novels describe as love?

If you do, my answer is a quick "no". This kind of love is not necessary because there have been thousands of happy marriages without it, from those in which the bridegroom was chosen for the bride (or vice versa) by elders, as was customary for centuries, down to the latest marriage of two young people who kept their wits about them all through their company-keeping and engagement.

The wild infatuation that some mistake for love is a minor form of hysteria, and hysteria is not only not necessary for, but a positive drawback to, a happy marriage.

But if you define love correctly, I say that it is absolutely necessary for a happy marriage. Love is an intelligent willingness to surrender self-will, to make sacrifices, to place fidelity, charity and duty above feelings, on behalf of a person whom one has found to be a good companion, a sturdy character, and a believer in the same purposes of life and marriage as oneself.

The degree of physical and emotional attraction behind this determination of the free will may vary greatly, but it is never the essence of love.

Too many young people have thought otherwise, to the effect that, with the inevitable lessening of infatuation after a year or two of married life, they have considered themselves no longer in love.

Love is a function of the free will, and it can last as long as the free will exercises itself according to the above definition.

Therefore, to say "I am in love" should mean "I am willing to surrender my will, to sacrifice my desires, to place duty and fidelity above all else, in behalf of one person whom I have found suitable for a successful marriage."

Is Love Sufficient for a Happy Marriage?

·Problem:

If one is deeply in love with a certain person, is not that sufficient for a happy marriage, even though others advise against the marriage?

I am in love with a young man, and want to marry him, but everybody tells me he won't make me happy. I am so happy just being in love with him that I know I'll be happy in marriage.

Solution:

It has been set down as one of the most futile things in life to argue with a young person already in love, who believes that the happiness of being in love is a true measure of the happiness that will be found in marriage.

However, those of us who are interested in the happiness of married folk will still go on trying to convince young people of the danger of this mistake.

You say that everybody tells you that the young man you love cannot make you happy in marriage.

I presume that this means your parents, your pastor or confessor, your close friends. Such unanimity can hardly be a result of conspiracy against you, or unfounded on good reasons.

With eyes undimmed by the infatuation that makes you a poor judge of your boyfriend, they must see something in his character that makes him unfit for the responsibilities of marriage.

Perhaps he is shiftless and undependable; perhaps a drunkard; perhaps unprincipled or irreligious.

After all, there are thousands of divorces in America each year, and tens of thousands of broken hearted wives.

Can't you see that most of the latter married because they were breathlessly in love, and only afterward, too late, found out that love is not sufficient for a happy marriage?

You did not tell me on what ground everybody opposes your marriage to this boy, and therefore I do not say for certain that their opposition is justified.

There is a good presumption that it is, however, from the fact that it is unanimous.

I do say firmly, however, that you are clinging to a false principle when you say that "because you are happy just being in love with your boyfriend, you know you'll be happy in marriage."

It takes more than love, I assure you, to make a marriage happy, and sometimes it is only your parents, pastor, and good friends, who can tell you whether that something is present or absent.

On Love at First Sight

Problem:

"Do you believe in love at first sight?

I recently met a man and fell head over heels in love with him on our first date. He seemed to feel the same way about me. If he asks me to marry him even after only three dates, I feel that I will just have to say *Yes*. Is not such a love sufficient to make marriage very happy?"

Solution:

No, it isn't, and if you look around, you will see hundreds of proofs of this fact. Love at first sight may be the preliminary to a happy marriage, but there is no guarantee that it will be.

I should say that the chances are definitely against a happy marriage, if love at first sight and three dates are the only preliminaries.

The reason should be clear: as a rational creature you are expected to use your head as well as your heart in all the important actions of your life.

There are few things more important than getting married, and once married, you are married till the death of either yourself or your partner.

This love at first sight that you talk about is an emotional reaction to someone who seems to have many fine qualities on the surface.

It cannot possibly see into the heart, into the conscience, into the will, into the past.

It is easily possible that a man for whom a girl would feel love at first sight would be able to present a very lovable appearance for a time, while under the surface he was harboring any number of vices and evils.

It takes time to find out whether a man has the interior qualities necessary to make a good husband and a happy marriage.

And it takes common sense on your part not to say such things as that "you would have to say *Yes* at once if he asked you to marry him on your third date together."

By that time you might not even have found out whether he was married before; whether he had an ungovernable temper; whether he was subject to epilepsy, melancholia or alcoholism.

Most of the divorces result from short courtships and so-called love at first sight. Don't be like the foolish ones of your generation.

If you like this man at first sight, remember that you must use second sight and third sight and twentieth sight to know whether you can have reasonable assurance that he won't be giving you black eyes in the second month of your marriage.

Love at first sight is all right if after six months of going with the person you find that he is as good inside as he is outside, and that you won't offend God or renounce God by marrying him.

Advice to a Young Woman: Pray, Pray and Pray. Also, be a **good woman**. Don't grow up **TOO FAST,** but **enjoy life as God brings it to you.** If you work on being the holiest **and most virtuous woman of God** you can be, your vocation will **become clear.**

15. LENT LESSONS FOR YOUR CHILDREN

The Year & Our Children: Catholic Family Celebrations for Every Season

In the Year and Our Children, Mary Reed Newland talks about teaching our children valuable lessons during the grace-filled time of Lent.

One practice she did with her own children is the Lima Beans for sacrifices. The beginning of Lent each child had their own pile of different colored lima beans (they had colored themselves) so they could differentiate from each other's beans. Every time a sacrifice was made they would put one of their own lima beans in the jar. When Easter came the number of lima beans was rewarded accordingly.

A sweet practice that would be fondly remembered by the kids as they grew into adulthood....

Some of her own thoughts as they journeyed through Lent:

The meditations for the Stations of the Cross are most fruitful if they relate to daily life some trial we are struggling with now.

For example, our Lord's silence when He was condemned to death, when He was tormented by the soldiers, or when He fell under the weight of the Cross – this can be related to that commonplace of childhood: bickering.

Bickering is a form of verbal cannibalism.

The one who holds out longer with his pecking at another is victor, having reduced the victim to tears, goaded him to losing his temper, striking, or some other form of retaliation, which is all reported as an unprovoked injustice as follows:

"But I didn't do anything. Nothing. I just said . ."

"I just said" is himself far more culpable, usually, than the poor soul he has goaded beyond endurance.

There is no real remedy for this but silence on the part of victims.

Abstinence from it on the part of attackers is the perfect solution, of course, but if someone does start, silence will stop him.

This, however, is awfully hard on the one who is silent, because this is how bickering goes (as if you didn't know):

"You pig. You took the biggest."

"I did not, and I'm not a pig."

"You are too."

"I am not."

"You are too. Pig!"

"I am not a pig. I'm not. I'm not a pig I'm not a pig I'm not a pig!"

"You are too. You are a pig you are a pig you are a pig."

"I'm not I'm not I'm not."

"You are you are you are."

This could go on for an hour if Mother didn't begin to froth at the mouth. Whereas the silence treatment winds up the conversation (if you can call it that) as follows:

"You pig. You took the biggest."

"I did not. And I'm not a pig."

"You are too."

Silence. In other words, you are a Pig.

O cruel silence …

But children well understand that no one is really a pig; this is only a game to see who can make the other lose his temper first.

It is ugly and mean; and the winner is usually the older child because he knows the extent of the younger's endurance.

Out of his own store of unavenged wrongs, he chooses this way to refresh a bruised ego. If we have taught them what our Lord said must be the very basis for our behavior, we have the point of departure.

"Whatsoever you do to the least of my brethren, you do it to me."

Learning this, we know what we must know in order to put meditations on the Passion together with events out of daily life and discover how to use them.

Then we can see – and children can see it – that to provoke a brother or a sister is to provoke Christ; to be silent under provocation is to be silent with Christ.

It is not good to make such accusations while saying the Stations, but rather to connect the meditations with these real problems (names of particular children omitted), and return to the principles when we are on the scene of abuses that we must correct.

"You are teasing Christ when you tease your brother. It is the same. 'Whatsoever you do....', He said.

You torment him just for the fun of it the way the soldiers tormented our Lord.

Yet you really love him, as you really love our Lord.

Keep these things in the front of your mind during Lent, and try to bite your tongue when you are tempted to unkindness.

Each time you keep from saying something unkind, it is a triumph of grace, and our Lord will strengthen you with grace for the next time.

There are powerful graces coming to us during Lent, and we must try to use them to rid ourselves of our faults so that on Easter we can be free of them, like the newly baptized are free of Original Sin."

Impossible? Not really, although it will probably take a lifetime to do it. But it is the goal, and especially during Lent it is the spirit of the preparation: to be as those newborn, on Easter morning.

If we are spectators to such a moral victory, we must be sure to congratulate the hero. "Darling, I heard N. today when he called you a pig and tried to make you angry. It was wonderful, the way you didn't answer back and only walked away.

You used silence the way our Lord used it, the way He wants you to use it. When you are silent in union with Him, you are growing in the likeness of Christ."

When Dominic Savio was silent before an unjust accusation, he shamed the other boys into admitting their guilt.

This is often the effect of heroic efforts to reach out to Christ and bear hurts with Him. Grace is the invisible ingredient in all these struggles for perfection.

For every honest effort, one may put a bean in the jar. There are beans for all kinds of things: no desserts, no jumping for the telephone (a genius in our midst suggested this to eliminate violent jostling, wrestling, racing, leaping, and tugging – an excruciating discipline); no complaining about anything; doing chores promptly; no weekly penny for candy, and many more, including that magnificent and most glorious of all: coming when called.

All who do this are known as St. Theresas.

Actually, when you scan the long list of them, they amount to what spiritual directors call the "interior mortifications."

Our mantel is bare this season except for the two candelabra with their twelve candles and the crucifix between them. Even the bread and the bakings speak to us of Lent. Crosses of seeds decorate the bread (because when you see the seeds, you remember about "die so you may live"), and on biscuit crusts and meat pies, symbols of the Passion are cut.

He Is Most Powerful Who Has Himself in His Power.
-Seneca

Each man caught in the embrace of materialism is a soul *IN DANGER OF HELLFIRE*, and each soul is **infinitely precious to God.** For those of us who are parents, the challenge is *TERRIBLE INDEED.* We have placed in our care for a few short years **precious immortal souls** who belong to God, whose destiny is AN ETERNITY IN AND WITH GOD, and who depend **entirely upon us** for the formation of a way of life that will lead them surely to God. **And woe to us if we fail in this charge.** – Mary Reed Newland

16. BOOK REVIEW – THE PRECIOUS BLOOD AND MOTHER PRAYER BOOK

This is a wonderful little prayer book that I have used all through my married life. The prayers are beautiful and the promises wonderful!

The following are a couple of examples of special prayers I have used a lot:

Our Lady of this House:

Mary, Virgin Mother of God, conceived without sin, we choose you today as the Queen and Mother of our home.

We ask you, through the Precious Blood of Jesus and your Immaculate Conception, to preserve us from sickness, fire and water, lightning and storms, from war and theft, from loss of faith and sudden death.

Bless and protect, O holy Virgin, all who live here and preserve us from every other temporal and spiritual misfortune. Amen

Memorare to Jesus, Mary and Joseph:

(Inexpressible graces have been received through the use of this prayer, which in one cry of confidence, links together those three most dear and holy names: – Jesus, Mary, Joseph.) Remember, Heart of my Jesus, Immaculate Heart of Mary, and you, oh glorious St. Joseph, that no one has ever had recourse to Your protection, or implored your assistance without obtaining relief. Animated with the like confidence, I come laden with the weight of my sins, to prostrate myself before You. Oh Merciful Heart of Jesus, Immaculate Heart of Mary, and you, oh glorious St. Joseph, reject not my petitions, but graciously here and grant them. Amen

Here are some titles of the many prayers:

-Prayer for Choosing a State in Life

-Act of Consecration to the Precious Blood and the Blessed Virgin for Children

-Memorare to St. Joseph (and many other beautiful prayers to that Glorious Saint)

-A Prayer in time of Affliction, Wars, Pestilence, etc.

-Beautiful Prayers to many Saints

….and many, many more. It is a small prayer book with approximately 150 pages. You will find it a superb companion to your prayer life. You can locate the prayer book online.

17. A MOTHER'S CROSS
BY THERESA WALKER

Through casual observation, one will usually find mothers feeling that they are somewhat lacking in the spiritual heroics of the saints. Not that mothers lack a cross….they have a very real cross that must be carried with perfect balance. Why then, the negative view?

Perhaps, when carried well, it usually goes unnoticed. Is there a mother who has not heard the belittling comments like, "Oh, I couldn't just sit home and do *nothing*!" Yet these same women consider themselves lofty for having abandoned their homes, husbands and children (should they even have any). They prefer instead the "glamor" of a career….one where they will be paid cold, heartless cash rather than the love of a family and graces from God.

Even when one can ignore the noisy opinions of the world, it is still easy to get discouraged. When a mother of little ones actually steals a few quiet moments for spiritual reading, what does she find? She may find tales of hermits devoting their every moment to prayer – but what of her children! Perhaps she will read of saints who lived on the Blessed Sacrament alone – yet she must carefully nourish the unborn baby of her womb! There are stories of the nuns who founded orphanages country wide – but the government would not allow her compassionate heart to adopt even one child ("they have enough of their own!").

Poor mother! Do not count yourself as lost to the opportunity of heaven! Often the hardest cross is one of humble, quiet submission. In a way, a mother's crosses are usually determined by others, whether it is her husband's directives, or her children's desires, or God's Will. She will not always have the luxury of choosing what she will do that day. Much of her time is spent seeing to the needs of those she must serve.

If done with patience and even willingly, we can make a beautiful cross of many of the frustrations of everyday life. This could be as "easy" as rising from sleep countless times during the night to see to our newborn's endless needs without sighing, "*Oh, why me?*" We can simply let our husbands "inconsideration" go unnoticed (yes, even without rolling our eyes!) when he forgets to call to say he'll be later than expected. And we could use Aunt Martha's unannounced and inconveniently timed visits as a lesson in humility while we calmly try to hide the dirty laundry baskets!

As far as mothers go, there are seldom any that one hears being bragged about…except for the occasional mother who has six children, the oldest is six, keeps a tidy house that looks like a page from a décor magazine, everything she does is handmade from food to gifts, etc. But this is not the norm and to try to compete with *her* would be to deny who God made *you*. It would be a far more virtuous approach to offer our little crosses and shortcomings to Our Lady and ask her to perfect them before presenting them to her Divine Son. After all, she earned the greatest crown of reward that a human could and was she not a mother who cared for her family and home?

So while looking for crosses this Lent, why not choose the ones that mothers so often carry but forget to offer to heaven? Seeing these duties as cook, nurse, teacher, judge, jury, cheerleader, farmer, entertainer, secretary, tailor, etc. as a cross just waiting to be carried a little bit better will make these duties into acts of love. They will help us to show that love of a mother that we wish our children to associate with Our Blessed Mother.

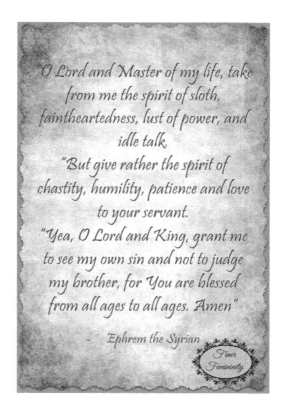

"O Lord and Master of my life, take from me the spirit of sloth, faintheartedness, lust of power, and idle talk.
"But give rather the spirit of chastity, humility, patience and love to your servant.
"Yea, O Lord and King, grant me to see my own sin and not to judge my brother, for You are blessed from all ages to all ages. Amen"

- Ephrem the Syrian

18. A SHORT, TALL TALE FOR MOTHERS BY THERESA WALKER

Once a young lady, by name of Veronica, was discerning her vocation. Feeling quite certain she was called to the vocation of marriage and motherhood, she began to fret that she was taking the "easy way" which would not be as pleasing to Our Lord.

Veronica's guardian angel appeared and asked her, "Why do you fear your vocation?"

"I fear not giving Our Lord the best cross I can carry. Isn't it a far greater cross that the religious life gives?" the poor girl asked.

Her angel took her to the village square and through his eyes she saw the crowd of passersby. First came a young man just starting to make his way in the world. On his shoulder, and without a tremendous struggle, he carried a modest-sized cross. "This is the cross he bears of his temptations to earn a dishonest living. But he was raised well, and so he handles the cross well," explained Veronica's angel.

Next came an innkeeper walking the other direction with no cross at all. "He threw away his cross years ago to live a life of sin," came the saddened angel's narrative.

Then came the local bishop. He was struggling under so great a cross that he was more crawling than walking. The bishop's guardian angel did the best he could to help the poor man onward. The gates of hell loomed just behind him. "But he will be crushed!" came the compassionate Veronica's cry.

"Not if he keeps striving forward," assured her angel.

The girl looked through the crowd for someone of her own resemblance who could help her indecision. She spotted some young ladies not far off. The first was a nun, newly professed and joyfully carrying a large cross of heavy, solid wood. Beside her walked her guardian angel, watching her, his sacred keep. Nearby were two young mothers. Both had a sack, one a very large and bulky bundle, the other a seemingly empty sack.

"Look, neither mother has a cross! They have nothing to give to Our Dear Savior!" was Veronica's disheartened thought.

"Look closer at the sacks," directed her angel.

Looking again at the mother with the large satchel, Veronica realized there was an innumerable cluster of little crosses in the sack. The burden was so great that the mother paused for a moment to try to regain her strength. The mother's own guardian angel was there to urge her on again and she continued through the square.

"But why is the other mother's sack empty?" asked Veronica as she watched the mother with the empty sack wander about the square. "Was she not given any crosses, great or small, to carry?"

"She is daily given a great number of little crosses but she chooses not to pick them up to carry for Sweet Jesus. Look even now," directed Veronica's tender angel.

The second mother's angel was holding out such a small cross for her it could have been held with ease. But the mother hardly even glanced at it. Instead she was distracted by the shops of the village square.

"You see," concluded Veronica's dear angel, "every person must find their cross in life. It may be a great one, it may be many small hidden ones, like the good mother's great sack. The size and number matters not. *How* you carry your cross, is what will please Our Dear Lord."

Veronica smiled and could sense her soul being called again to the married life. With a look of understanding and approval, her beloved guardian angel handed her an empty sack to fill.

19. TWO GREAT TIME-TESTED RECIPES

Basic Whole Wheat Bread

This is a great basic whole wheat bread recipe. I make 4 loaves at a time in my Bosch mixer. It turns out wonderful…every time!

Yields 5-6 loaves

2/3 C honey
2/3 C oil
6 C warm water
3 TB Instant Yeast
1 1/2 – 2 TB Real Salt
16-20 C fresh whole wheat flour
3 TB Dough Enhancer
1/3-1/2 Cup Vital Wheat Gluten

I often do not use the gluten and sometimes even leave out the dough enhancer.

After kneading, form into loaves and let rise in greased loaf pans. Bake@ 350 degrees for 45 minutes.

GRANOLA:

We use this recipe a lot. In the brackets are the measurements I use for a large and hungry family! Even then it doesn't last long enough! :)

3 cups oats   (12 cups)

1/2 cup flour, barley or whole wheat   (2 cups)

1/3 cup sunflower seeds   (1 1/2 cups)

1/3 cup sesames seeds, hulled   (1 1/2 cups)

1/3 cup almonds, slivered   (1 1/2 cups)

1/4 cup pecans   (1 cup)

1/2 tsp. cinnamon, ground   (2 tsp.)

1/4 tsp.nutmeg, ground   (1 tsp.)

1/4 tsp. sea salt   (1 tsp.)

1/4 cup maple syrup – or other liquid sweetener   (2 cups)

1/4 cup canola oil   (1 cup…I use a mixture of melted butter and light tasting oil from the health store)

1 tsp. vanilla extract   (4 tsp.)

Directions:

1. Mix dry ingredients.

2. Mix liquid ingredients and stir into the dry ingredients.

3. Spread on lightly oiled cookie sheet. Bake at 275 degrees until done. Stir every 10 minutes. Watch so it doesn't burn.

I add my dried fruit after the granola cools off (raisins, dried blueberries, etc.)

20. THE FAMILY AND THE CROSS

RT. REV. MSGR. IRVING A. DEBLANC, 1958

ASK MOTHERS AND fathers if they would like to become saints. Many apologetically answer, "Would that I had the time! I am too busy rearing the children, keeping house, making ends meet." This recalls the days when some considered sanctity a luxury for the rich, who in being able to afford servants, could spend long hours in church and in prayer: they were often considered to be the holy ones.

Pope Benedict XV defined holiness as "doing the will of God according to one's state of life." In the state of grace and with the right intention, married people can become saints doing their everyday home work. They often gain more graces with a dish cloth than with a Rosary, as one may sometime gain more graces getting up in the middle of the night to care for a baby than spending an hour in church.

It is a matter of doing the right thing at the right time. Yes, but even more, it is fulfilling a sacramental vocation. This cannot be said in the same sense about being a lawyer, or a secretary, or a farmer. Marriage is a vocation; it is holy; it is a sacrament; it is a means of going to heaven.

It is interesting that only three of the sacraments are entitled "holy": Holy Eucharist, Holy Orders, Holy Matrimony--not that the others are not holy but these are specifically designated. As a priest gets graces when he hears confessions, preaches, reads his breviary, so a couple under the right conditions is flooded with God's graces when they love each other, nurse a baby, teach the children.

This because they too are fulfilling their vocation. It is because more and more people see marriage as a vocation that we can hope for more and more saints among those living family life.

In Peru four natives have already been canonized and one beatified in a hundred years. In the U.S.A. so far we still have had no natives canonized. I am afraid we are not even remotely thinking in the direction of trying to be worthy to be a canonized saint.

Married couples are sometimes unaware that suffering is one of their great home-made tools for sanctity. It is looked upon as an annoyance, but Christian marital love necessarily involves suffering, for the essence of unity is not so much to enjoy each other, but to suffer together. Still joy and suffering are not two sides of a unity called love. What was once "desire" before marriage becomes "offering" after marriage. Some have described love as having three aspects: the digestive, the reciprocal, and the oblative. It is in the "oblative" sense, this self-giving and suffering that a couple purifies love.

Without these elements, love would die, for passion can only promise, love can keep that promise. To refuse the call of self-immolation is the "sin" of obduracy and a rejection of love. One is then of no use to God, to society, to each other, or to oneself. To say "no" to this human impulse is to corrupt all one touches. It is the cult of selfishness. The Cross can teach us to love our neighbor; it can teach us compassion. Three-fourths of us, it is said, need it, but there is a strange, unhappy feeling that in too many souls this ingredient is left out.

The Cross is our main tool of sanctity at home. Christian love understands the Cross if it is seen in the context of Heaven. For pagans the Cross is a scandal. It absorbs them like whirlpools in a river at flood height. Suffering, however, must draw men outside of themselves. It is a reminder of Divinity itself. Not good in itself, the Cross can be priceless as a means of grace.

The bell rings in the life of every one of us and all of us are someday called upon to suffer. The non-Christian tries to escape suffering and he becomes hard and selfish. He seeks comfort only and his spiritual energy dries up, but he must learn to suffer or it will destroy him. The egotist detaches himself from spiritual reality and becomes a hollow being--an empty body. Like the statue of Buddha, he looks down only at his own stomach and does not see the needy around him.

Not all can see the value of suffering. Suffering is often so inward, so hard to articulate. It has been a special mystery to all, especially pagans. Their many explanations have never been satisfactory.

The Stoic saw in suffering a test of sheer courage; he was completely indifferent to it. The Epicurean saw his answer in pleasure, and the Dolorist tried to delude himself and saw evil as good and actually exulted in that which diminished him. Others saw in suffering only a mere punishment.

A good Catholic makes friends with pain. He holds God's gifts close to himself but always with open hands. When God allows us sufferings it is not "to do us harm but to gather us into His arms." Suffering never gags a Christian, upon it he sharpens his teeth.

Like a cargo stabilizing a ship against storms, so suffering stabilizes us against the storms of passion. Humanity will ever question suffering, as Job did so dramatically and so officially. But Job gave an answer. Pagan philosophers never learned it. Christ gave the answer for all times: suffering calls less for a philosophy, more for a living of it as worthwhile.

"So vast was this question," says Paul Claudel, the great convert to Catholicism, "that the Word alone could answer it, but He did so not by an explanation, only by His presence." This presence helped Mary who stood beneath the first Red Cross crimsoned by the blood of her Son; it helped Veronica who so lovingly held a cool, moist compress to the throbbing, fevered brow of Christ; it helped Simon of Cyrene, who later gave his life to serve others, this same Simon must have seen the pallid face of Christ among the poor and on every crumpled pillow where a sick man's head lay.

We learn with St. Francis de Sales that the love of Jesus begins in the Passion. We learn with Bishop Neumann of the deep beauty of the Litany of the Sacred Heart--a prayer he vowed to say every day. With St. Alphonsus we become more conscious of the Cross. It is constantly in his writing. When he saw a nail, a rope, a thorn, he thought instantly and tenderly of the Passion. The Cross returns us to the nothingness that we are and yet it lifts us into eternity. With Abraham Lincoln we fall on our knees often with the realization that there is no one else to go to.

In many churches of the country a large, special cross is carried in church for the Stations. There is no corpus on the cross; each person is reminded that he must replace Christ on the cross. He must learn how to suffer and why he suffers. He must be an extension of Christ.

Christ has plunged Himself into humanity and wants us to make Him real today. He wants us to continue His Redemption, but this is done not by writing a good book, or organizing well, or by a great oration. One is a Christian when he or she represents Christ, "witnesses" Christ.

Deeply we surrender our will, not with a mere external offering like that of Cain, but with an internal-external oblation like that of Abel--like that of Christ. The external gift is a symbol of the internal giving. We represent Christ so perfectly that we become a mystery to those around us.

In the everyday romance of the world we pierce our valentines with an arrow. The Sacred Heart is the first, true Valentine sent by the Father. But His love is pictured by a heart and a cross rather than an arrow. His heart is not only the symbol of love but the Cross of hope.

The Cross is not the symbol of death; it is the symbol of life. The Stations do not end with a dead Christ in the tomb, but a glorious, living Christ on Easter Sunday, and always in our tabernacles. He is every city's most distinguished resident who invites His best friends constantly to "take up your Cross and follow Me."

The Cross is Christ's way of identifying Himself and His own. Christians realize it is a gift, not a curse for with Dante "sorrow remarries us to God."

"When we abandon all to Him, He takes a tender care of us, and His Providence for us is great or small according to the measure of our abandonment."
St. Francis de Sales

21. LOVE – CHRIST IN THE HOME

By Father Raoul Plus, S.J., 1950's

Why does a woman desire a man? Why does a man desire a woman? What is the explanation of that mysterious attraction which draws the two sexes toward each other?

Will anyone ever be able to explain it? Will anyone be able to exhaust the subject?

One fact is certain: Even aside from the physiological aspect of the problem, the effeminate man does not attract a woman; she makes fun of him, finds him ridiculous. So too the masculine woman weakens her power of attraction for a man, and ends by losing it entirely.

The age-old spell which each sex casts upon the other is closely allied to the fidelity with which each exactly fulfills its role. If woman copies man and man copies woman, there can be comradeship but love does not develop. In reality, they are nothing more than two caricatures, the woman being degraded to the rank of a man and a second-rate man at that, and the man to the rank of a manikin in woman's disguise. The more feminine a woman's soul and bearing, the more pleasing she is to a man; the more masculine a man's soul and bearing, the more pleasing he is to a woman.

We do not mean to say that between two poor specimens of either sex there will never be any casual or even lasting sexual appeal and experience. But we can hardly, if ever, call it love. If men and women are no more than two varieties of the same sex, a sort of neuter sex, the force which creates love disappears. Normally, as we say in electrical theory, opposite charges must exist before any sparks will shoot forth. Bring into contact two identical charges and there will be no effect; electricity of opposite polarities must be used; then and then only will there be reaction.

In the realm of love, the general rule is the same. In fact, man and woman are two different worlds. And that is as it should be, so that the eternal secret which each of them encloses may become the object of the other's desire and stimulate thirst for a captivating exploration.

That is love's strange power. It brings two secrets face to face, two closed worlds, two mysteries. And just because it involves a mystery, it gives rise to limitless fantasies of the imagination, to embellishments in advance of the reality. So that **one finally loves all toward which one rows.**

Whether that toward which one rows is an enchanted island or one merely believes it is, what ecstasy!

Comes the meeting, the consecration of the union by marriage; each brings to the other what the other does not possess. In the one, delicate modesty and appealing reserve; in the other, conquering bravery. A couple has been born. Love has accomplished its prodigy.

Yet, how true it is, that having said all this, we have said nothing. The reality of love is unfathomable.

Could it be perhaps because it is the most beautiful masterpiece of God?

"Marriage has been chosen as the image of the perfect union between the soul and Christ because in marriage, likewise, the center and core is love. No other earthly community is constituted so exclusively in its very substance by mutual love."

-Dietrich von Hildebrand

22. EASTER ALLELUIAS

The Year & Our Children: Catholic Family Celebrations for Every Season - Mary Reed Newland

This is, for me, the most beautiful of all the Easter stories.

It should be the very last thing at night, after prayers, for the little ones. Ours have heard it as they lay in their beds.

It is about Mary Magdalene and how she found Him in the garden on Easter morning. She did not really understand. After all He had said about rising on the third day, still she wept and wrung her hands and looked for Him.

Even when she saw the angels, it did not dawn on her. Then – she saw Jesus. Thinking He was a gardener, she heard Him say, "Woman, why art thou weeping? For whom art thou searching?"

And she said, "If it is thou, Sir, that hast carried Him off, tell me where thou hast put Him, and I will take Him away."

Then that lovely moment. He said simply, "Mary." And she knew.

How tender, the love that inspired them to record this scene. We know that He appeared to His Mother first. It is an ancient tradition in the Church, and St. Teresa of Avila and many others confirm it.

But for us who are sinners, the scene described so carefully is this meeting with the one who was such a great sinner. It should be a part of every child's Easter Eve, and often it will make them weep.

But these are fine, good tears, that come because they understand that He loves them.

Alleluia at Last

Easter morning. Alleluia!

The Hallel, greatest of Hebrew expressions of praise, together with Jah, the shortened form of Jahve, God's name, combine to make this lovely word.

Dom Winzen writes: On the eve of Septuagesima Sunday, the Alleluia was buried. Now it rises out of the tomb…. The Alleluia is the heart of the Opus Dei; the song which the Moses of the New Testament sings together with His People after He has passed through the Red Sea of His Death into the glory of His Resurrection.

The first child awake races downstairs! Quickly they all gather and at last the door to the living room is opened.

There are the marvelous baskets, resplendent with decorations, with gifts, with goodies. Walk carefully. The eggs are hidden everywhere.

All together sing another Alleluia! as the early one lights the Paschal candle.

Then to Mass, to the great joy of Easter Communion. He is in each of us; therefore we are one in Him.

At every Mass, He will be our Paschal Lamb, the perfect sacrifice, the perfect victim, offered everywhere for us, always, until the world comes to an end.

Home to the beautiful breakfast table, the delicious Easter bread, the excitement of the egg hunt, and the opening of gifts.

It has been so long since we have sung Alleluia after Grace. What a glorious morning!

The Paschal candle is lighted. While we rejoice, it burns with a steady flame. It says, "I am risen, and am still with thee, Alleluia!"

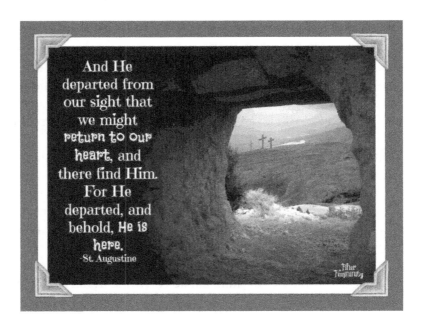

And He departed from our sight that we might return to our heart, and there find Him. For He departed, and behold, He is here.
-St. Augustine

THE
Time-Warp
Wife

When I yield
my will, my desires,
and my passions for
the good of my family,
I yield myself to the
will of *God.*

— Darlene Schacht

23. SMORGASBORD 'N' SMIDGENS

Hats were "in" this winter, thanks to Virginia's crocheting efforts!

Warm hugs for Grandpa!

Big Smiles for Mom & Dad. Jeanette is expecting #2!

Margy, Rosie and I just back from Church.

Regina & Michelle VanderPutten, Hillarie George with lovely smiles!

Colin and Z....a special couple!

A dear friend, Natalie Porter, with little Benedict.

Natalie's children are having a great time with those sophisticated and expensive children's toys........boxes!

Natalie's kitchen....Rachel & Francesca getting ready for Easter!

Natalie and her children. Natalie is expecting # 10!

Gemma wrote and directed her little play, "Tarcisius".

Tarcisius gets pummeled with "stones"!

Father prays for the dying Tarcisius.

Brendan & Sienna, sweet grandchildren

Mary Ann Scheeler, author of the article "Cloth, Fabric, Style" with her children.

Mary Ann, hiking & visiting at Mystic Lake with her children.

My dear dad passed away Nov. 18th. He is missed.

His death and his funeral were beautiful, full of the richness of our faith!

My mom, Beulah, and I

T.J. & Theresa Walker and Family. Theresa authored the articles "A Mother's Cross" and "A Short, Tall Tale for Mothers". T.J. is the brother of Father Walker, FSSP (below) who was murdered June 11, 2014. Father was a dear friend...

Father Kenneth Walker, FSSP, R.I.P. (Bottom photo taken by Larry Katsbulas)

Good friends, Isabel & Rachel Bogowith with Isabel's mother, Evelyn Shibler

Anthony & Isabel Bogowith with Caleb and Rachel

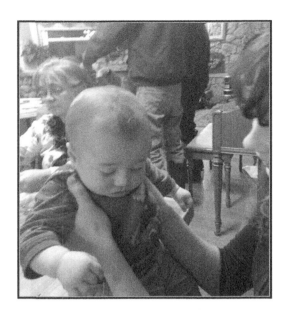

Please Nathaniel, WAKE UP!!

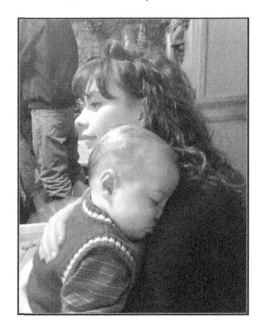

Oh, forget it.....

Aprons on and ready to go to work! Below: Margy and Rosie

We even get the guys to work around here!

Puzzles, games and just good, wholesome FUN!

Choir Practice for the Traditional Family Weekend.

Gary & Rosalie (Jeanette's mom and dad-in-law) visit from Maine!

Good Fathers…. Top: Fran VanderPutten from Missouri

Bottom: Gerard Billington with Baby Tristan from New Zealand

Our family at my dad's wake. We look happy....we were. Dad had a holy
death and in spite of knowing we would miss him, we were content.

Chillin' at Grandma's

Nice spring days!

Christian joy is a gift of God flowing from a good conscience.

~St. Philip Neri

Take time to smell the flowers this spring!

To keep posted on upcoming issues of Finer Femininity Publications subscribe to the email notifications at Finer Femininity Website:
www.finerfem.wordpress.com

ABOUT THE AUTHOR

Hello! My name is Leane VanderPutten.

My family and I live in rural Kansas. Married 29 years, my husband, Vincent, and I have 11 children and (almost) 18 grandchildren. Our family strives to be faithful to Our Lord and His Church. We are devoted Catholics, homeschoolers, with 6 children still at home.

Our married children live nearby and we see our grandchildren often. Our family life is lively, full of faith and joy, with the occasional hardship sprinkled in.

My focus here, at **Finer Femininity,** is on the family — becoming the best possible wives and mothers. There is much in the church and in the world today to cause confusion and anxiety. We must bring up our children to thrive in a world full of this discord, with that inner peace only He can bring. This serenity is a fundamental part of the solution to all our troubles.

Here we learn ways to enhance our relationships. We learn about tweaking our attitudes. Often we need a paradigm shift in the way we look at circumstances to manage them in a manner more pleasing to God. The journey is uphill, sometimes rocky, often steep, but always edifying.

It is an inspiring work for me to share this information with all of you, and to reach more deeply into my own heart so I may change in order to become a better wife and mother, and especially, daughter of Him who sustains me every day on my journey.

May God bless us and Our Lady guide us as we endeavor to make this world a better place for our children and for our society, one day at a time.

Made in United States
Orlando, FL
12 August 2024

50284023R00068